Blue Maze

Poems, 2019

Rosemary Ybarra-García

Produced in United States of America

Chayo Press, 2019
P.O. Box 3691
Half Moon Bay, CA 94019

Cover Image: Sofia Isabel Fillon

for Alfonso

Table of Contents

Blue Marble

My earliest memory—two rough hands
yearning to hold me, a flowered dress
clinging to a thick body,
tears dripping from exhausted eyes

It was a ragged world of muddy boots,
sweat and laughter,
    where I felt safe

As the earth moved
to collect us,
I began to understand:
    death took people away,
    those near me worried,
    faces of strangers frightened me

While still young enough to
escape imaginary villains
in a speeding wagon,
    I swallowed a blue marble,
    a talisman, found in the dirt

It was a part of me for many years,
tugging at me, waiting for me to acquiesce
to the earth's capricious currents
    as she shifted for balance
    on a swiftly moving wagon

Rain

I inhale the width
of the earth, seagulls

slice through air, swells
slap
jagged bluffs

I am rain, falling through
thirsty skies

I moisten feathers, spray
rocks, hardened
by time

Years of living
flow
through my fingers

My heart endures
the raspy voice of storm clouds,
the tumbling
limbs of dead trees

The earth absorbs
me as I land, assimilates me
into her burrow, filled with

grains of sand, so intimate, yet
so detached in minute worlds

It is a dense view
against my
liquid perspective, my

need to breathe freely, my
transparency

Tide Pools

I jump over tide pools

The scent of sea urchins,
warbling seaweed
explodes
over stark white shells,
blue green pools, black turban snails

A womb of
amethysts and emeralds
opens
to the hatching life

A smiling sea anemone
dances
in and out
of turquoise fairy gardens,

asking for nothing more

Blue Vase

Slim silk,
hourglass neck,
brush strokes
of midnight blue

She is a cool clandestine
walk on sand,
ocean waves
in silver moonlight

The jealous rain, in its
cerulean sheen,
its transparency,
stares through a window,
beyond an overcast
living room,

beyond a tan Persian carpet,
to the mantle,
to white Asiatic lilies in piano hands,

to the blueness
of a long neck, a full mouth,
deep curves

The Apatheia of Stones

I want to be like stones
They do not suffer passions, make
careless judgments

They are steadfast and never panic,
love in serpent moves,
take their time to touch,

unlike flesh, organic emotions;
unlike brain-matter love—analytical,

hypocritical, hysterical;

unlike rapid kisses, fast-moving feet
in and out of relationships,
fleeing at lizard speed

I Often Look Behind Things...

to see what lies

behind
a chair,
the façade of a building,
old road signs

behind
the backs of bent shoulders,
beneath a hot August sky,
picking and packing
their future
one piece at a time

behind
anger that dwells
in knotted ropes,
craving to be heard

behind
my *own* perspective of things
where hypocrisy may linger
beyond my vision, where desires
may hide in corners

Lamp in a Window

Lonely as
a serenade in snow,

two pair of eyes
converge on a page

Voyeurs peer
through the cool night air
as stars shift

A couple reaches for
glasses of red wine,
warmth of fire, wordless talk,
eloquent touches,
fever of escape

into an untitled book
still without a cover

Dance of the Cypress Tree

Lady ferns sway,
   a ballerina pirouettes
      against an orange sun

A tree clutches the bluff,
      overlooks the world

A shy moon,
   a yoga sunset
      swallow daylight

She twists, turns
   in playful puffs of air
      with a hint of naughtiness,

      for if she could, she would
         dance upon ocean waves,
            over mountains

      to find, at last, the one
         who left her with this yearning,
            this indelible longing

      to rip her roots from the earth,
         fly among birds and gusts of wind

Folded Secret

I folded a secret
that cannot be undone
into a copy of Wuthering Heights

A secret that nagged like a shadow
on dark nights,
slashed peaceful dreams

To a woman's secret
of thorns and red roses,

I have said good-bye,
buried it in a book,

a book dripping
of ancient grief,
intense lovers,

who emerge at death
from a gothic fog
of redemption

Lace and Faith

When she moved, she left
laced heirlooms and her faith behind—

the yellowed, crocheted tablecloth, its arms unravelling;
black laced scarves, folded forever in a drawer,

worn by widows at funerals and graveyards,
by a doña who turned the unfaithful to stone

Stern, pale faces stayed behind with tablecloths,
dusty doilies, strict religious hardness

They all stayed behind despite their pleas
for a spot in the moving van

Faith, being so persistent, would find its way,
traveling through miles of countryside,

stopping for water, leaving its stamp,
a bit of itself everywhere

It would cry at the front door until she let it inside
It would not look like the old faith—fat and balding,

wearing a monk's cassock from the sixteenth century,
wooden rosaries hanging from his waist

No, at first, it would be as unassuming as a kitten,
mewing its way into her house

To My Ovaries

You have shrunken
They tell me you are but a spot
on a mariner's chart
When did you begin to shrink?
Was it when I no longer
wrote in metaphors?

Perhaps it was when the sculpture
in the stone garden
no longer amused me,
when the ocean of work seduced me,
when I became a single spray in its waves?
Was it then, I began to dry up
like the wild grasses of summer?

From the inside out,
the cynical laugh began
in the small of my uterus
No one heard the foreboding melody
as its long fingers reached
for juicy plums and morning flowers

I did not hear it
as I waltzed over sand dunes,
picked wild marigolds in the spring;
I did not hear it from the face
in the velvet mirror,
nor did I hear it
in my love's laugh

It was not until they told me
you had shrunken
that I heard the song
creep from within

Scattered Stones

Temple of Baalshamin, Palmyra, Syria,
17 A.D.-2015

The scent of war lingers
among corners of faith,
arches of worship

Eyes of statues cry upon
inverted steeples,
vacant altars supplicate
Byzantine skies for clemency

Wine of life
drips upon
roads of fire, leaving
footprints of ghostly forms
in hunched obedience

Fallen pillars
hide the baby Jesus,
tangled in the arms
of Mohammad and Baal

Stones, stones, everywhere,
hardened by something
longer than time,
older than war

There is Something in the Air

The scent of dissension
plagues the perennials of spring

Crumbling petals
cling to frail stamens

Blooms of chrysanthemums
threaten not to resurrect

The whippoorwill sings
in a nagging, steady beat

Spring wears gossamer in winter;
winter wears wool in summer

Waiting for Spring

Ironweed and smooth aster
recoil blossoms and transform to dry weeds
Like love that flowers and fills the heart,
they too soon fold into melancholy commonness—
with few blooms and faded shades of gray

I am a weed on the dry, hot plains
There inside, my seeds wait for spring,
cling to the parched earth,
crack and split to dust,
suck the earth, every cell petrified

Remainder

After leaving a bit
of me here and there,

shedding the breath of
my bones
on a lonely beach,

I am left with a thin veneer
wavering over skinny passions,
frail opinions, weak as
puffs of dandelions

I spent you my friends of youth,
when I was less prepared,
less thoughtful,

running with yearlings,
knotty knees crossing
over words, blushing my way
through that time

when our ideas
were on boundless
journeys, trekking
through the crispness
of new trails

Quietus

Echoes of wailing wind
send warnings
through the dense forest

Sunlight slices through blank spaces,
falls upon the musty crumbs

of autumn. Winter resonates
through spines of eucalyptus and pine,
casts tremors within creatures

tethered

between the orange calm of fall,
the biting chill of winter

Colors sprout wings;
stark whiteness smothers
the forest floor

Prints in snow
cross the meadow;
the "pale rider" gallops
over powdery clouds

A thin layer of gray
obscures the landscape;
an opaque lens reflects
a dream—untouchable and distant

The roar of winter
renders mute

the sound of a breaking branch,
a falling acorn

Rented Space

From an invisible point
to the present time
in the nook
of this rented space,

I am prefabricated seeds,
sprout wings,
cling to bracken fern,
fold inward,
prance with seasons,

drink rain,
inhale
the scent of honeysuckle,
wilt into the earth,

return—a grain of sand,
a breath of carbon, a whiff of nitrogen

Tapestry

In this house,
I interlace pieces left behind,

        broken strands, holes filled with
        blended cultures,
            rags of divergent voices

I throw out dust balls,
        uncover the mistress of color,
        wrapped in a teal scarf,
            braided into wings

I have woven a motley tapestry—
        of bright hues,
            a mix of threads

Counting

One by one
fireflies
evoke a shift
in time

Wings flutter,
each trill
a microsecond

Untouched thoughts
disappear
into a swirl
of branches

One by one,
years flit by
into beads
of consciousness

I count drips
of water
as they fall
from the garden faucet

I should rise
from this bench,
run through
my lists

Instead, I linger
in this world

of dragonflies fluttering
back and forth,
a spider spinning its web,
two birds
quarreling over dinner

...
Counting assures me
things
are as they should be

Meditation

My shallow breath ripples
over waves, waits
for a steady hum

        I do not fear the
        unfurnished darkness, deafness
        of noise, hunger of color

Providence
will write
my final step

        I welcome her as a mysterious woman in black
        who walks through the night
        with a machete in one hand
        a white dove in the other

Tonight, I am humbled
when stars bare smiles
upon the willow tree in the yard
and the house adjusts to groans of its arthritic bones

Alone, in this inner wilderness, I begin
to see her as a river, changing
direction with every shift of the earth

Etude

I acquiesced
to Chopin's shifting
melancholy,
his haunting base,
erotic tones

I saw a glimpse
of his internal glow—
falling scales, crashing
thunder bolts,
rushing arpeggios

I loved his trills,
thin filigree of sound,
laced voices
in sparrow wings

Like a moth,
I flittered over keys,
modulated
into popular lyrics

The melody between us
became
dissonant...

when I ceased
to love him properly

Volcanic Mountain

I stand in awe
of the earth's sorrow,
embrace the barren beauty

of her black, sharp rocks
her bubbling fire

Anger pours over oozing sores,
snakes to the amber ocean
in livid, molten rock

I learn who I am not;
who I never was

She erases my name,
as puddles of earth,
pieces of bone assimilate
into dark triangles of space

Wheat Field

Yellow silk
swings upwards
in angular reaches

Pulsing fingers
play upon
amber rustlings

Freshly washed sheets
surrender
as the capricious wind
changes course;

a chorus of gawking crows
retreats to the spoils
of shifting storms

Like wheat, I arc
the sheath of my back,
bending
with currents
of wavering squalls

Ocean

Sand caresses my heels,
rushes through my toes,
surrounds my ankles

As I reach the water, the ocean
encases my feet, studies them for
silver scales, fins, bulging eyes

It is irrelevant
that I am a finless creature;
the sea will accept me if I enter
its blue reach and will slowly
devour me, for it is,
as I am, a thing that devours
We have this in common

I am a nematode-like creature
burrowing into the earth's breath,
tipping its axis

The Rose That Held Us

The rose, hollow
in her beauty,
held us close
to her breasts
with thorny words,
hypnotic petals

When her anger sent
us scurrying
to corners of a nearby field,
we hid among wild grasses
and wished to run away

We hated wearing
crocheted hats,
made with thorny hands,
eating charred meat and
overcooked vegetables

Like budding squash
and spreading thyme,
at last we emerged
full bloom

After flying over valleys,
mountains without borders,
we returned
to her wilted bosom,

watered her
with a thinness
of breath and a plethora
of regrets

The Wick of Us

Fire on blackness,
candles lead us
through a labyrinth
of darkness

Horizontal or vertical,
flames seek sky,
softly light
a dinner for two,
a dark hallway

Braided knives
cut through
folded thoughts,
show the way
to the light

At their final breath,
smoldering wicks,
like us, balance
between extinction
and redemption

The Rhythm of Grass

I love those days
when the bulrush grew
    in rhythms
    with foxtail and meadow fescue;
when blankets of thin fingers
    reached from the ethereal earth
    to the salient sun,
    danced with the supple, warm wind;
when we children raced through slender leaves,
    caressed the grass as if it were a playmate;
when the damp yellow scent
    covered the plains
and that sticky-to-the-tongue taste filled us

Beach House

This house of meshed wire,
concrete, and glue

was created in a web
of a mind
with many tangles and turns

This house, a church
where tears, anger, laughter

fly like finches
through its branches

Long gone are swear words
written on its bones,

as this house now beckons me
to call upon the seeds
of my birth

I dwell in this *hogar*
among raspberries and sage,
squash and roses,

sit behind Mecho Shades,
under lamps of glass and iron,
on floors of cement

Cement, gray and cracked,
should be cold,
should emit unwelcome vibrations,

but instead, is warm
like old shoes
wearing scars of living,

a peaceful stream
by a copse of birch trees

If I let it, it will take me
where I need to go—

to a muse,
beyond concrete thoughts,
beyond grazing in the unconscious,

where lulling groans
of the ocean and
tales of lost fishermen
carry me away

Earth Warrior's Flute

"Zuni Sunrise" flows
across the sky
with soul tones

Clarity slides deep
into the bedrock
of my consciousness

A presence in
lingering blue streaks
traverses the horizon

A young warrior
remembers grandfathers,
ponders creation

Drums,
shaman-like voices
announce Wolf Mother

As the sun rises,
wild horses
cross the plains

The Girl Who Never Was

The woman felt the girl's gaze
from behind a screen door,
an ageless child, a body of mist,
wearing fibers of broken time

She stood on that indecisive
bough for a pat on the head,
a ribbon of remembrance,
quickly fading

What had held her bones, her soul there?

Searching for her
through the broken door,
up stairways of time,

the woman knew
the girl was the stain
that never was, a shadow with
an insatiable hunger to be

I know I am Repeating Things

Tomorrow,
I will stop annoying
the air between us,
the sedentary
fog that separates us

There can be no
walking backwards,
no starting over

Spring is a time for lovers

I stretch the branch of my hand
over mountains of foliage
that took so long to plant

You wince
at the crevices,
the patterns on my face

There will be
no repetition
of our springtime rain

Tomorrow,
I will stop waiting
for spring;
instead,
I will love the warm
embraces of winter

The Interruption

Branches shiver
as the forest
fills with a melody
that tip toes

across a creek
in the skin of a deer,
trills in the twitter
of a male thrush

When popping sounds
pierce through trees,
death rises
in silhouettes of smoke,
silence flees
in a stern staccato song

Wet shoes, dry leaves,
feathers, mud
cross the forest floor

until a single note
returns
in a fine dirt trail

Pneuma...

a gentle breath
illuminating jellyfish
in the ocean,
fireflies
in the garden

Father

was tomatoes from dusty fields,
was the cotton that pricked his fingers

He held the earth close;
the earth held him closer

Tolerant of sloppy
thinkers and wide-eyed teens,

he sparked in us an intense fire
to imagine

gateways through fences,
pathways through forests

Downdraft

flashes of time
flow in a downdraft:

She is standing at the kitchen sink
washing scraps off unmatched plates

She moves from one chore to another,
from one room to another,

to the garden, in a frenzy
of fixing, folding, ferreting away

She spits out chilling commands
as we wait on our shelves—

two dolls in pretty dresses,
dusted off and fed

In a puff of time, we
leave with a squall of expectations

When we return, I revisit these memories
like a zephyr, not wanting to disturb

a young mother whose monsoon
arrived before her first inspiration

Mask in the Mirror

A red-lipped smile
screens out thoughts,
too busy for reflection

Memories hide under
black eyeliner,
false eyelashes

Thick Cover Girl makeup
veils old gossip,
weary eyes

Hairline fissures meander
like a river from nostrils
to corners of a mouth

Through these cracks,
shadows of decay
allude
to a certain beauty
ignored

Blessed is the Dawn

The swelling sun flushes morning
out of its reverie,
peacock feathers shimmer
over drowsy rooftops,
doors and sunflowers open
to blaring early rays,
cock doodle-doodles
sing over backyard fences,
the scent of coffee snakes
through a cascade of "to do" lists,
hurried headlights push
toward the smile of day

Blessed is the dawn!

Acknowledgements

Thankful acknowledgement to those publications in which poems from BLUE MAZE were first published: "To my Ovaries," *Poetry Quarterly*, Prolific Press, 2013; "Quietus," *Poetry Quarterly*, Prolific Press, 2014; "Beach House," *California Quarterly*, California State Poetry Society, 2016; "Faith and Lace," *Calyx Journal*, Calyx Press, 2017; "Scattered Stones," *California Quarterly*, California State Poetry Society, 2017; "Lamp in the Window," *River Poets Journal*, Lily Press, 2017; "Blue Vase," *Minute Magazine*, Minute Press, 2019; Poem, "Rain," nominated for Pushcart Poetry Prize by California State Poetry Society, 2016.

Special thanks to Coast Writers at Café Society, to Diane Moomey and Shirley Holley for their suggestions, to Andres García for his thoughtful comments and support, and to writers from Odd Fellows of Half Moon Bay, California..

Biography

Rosemary is an educator and a lifelong poet who has been a featured poet for several years at coffee shops, book stores, women's study classes, and special venues such as "Women and the Muse" in Santa Cruz, CA, 1988; "Floricanto in Xochitle in Cuicatle, Flower and Song" at the De Young Memorial Museum in San Francisco, CA, 1993.

Her poetry has been included in several publications, among those: *Lighthouse Point*: An Anthology of Santa Cruz Writers, M PRESS, Santa Cruz, CA; *New to North America:* Writing by Immigrants, Their Children and Grandchildren, Burning Bush Publications, Santa Cruz, CA; *California Quarterly*, A California State Poetry Society Publication; *Poetry Quarterly,* Prolific Press Publication; *Calyx Journal*, CALYX Press; *River Poets Journal*, Lily Press; *Minute Magazine*, Minute Press.